Baby Animals

Written and Illustrated by Karen Rissing

Modern Publishing
A Division of Unisystems, Inc.
New York, New York 10022

Printed in Singapore

Foal

Goslings

Lambs

Calf

Chicks

Each day, baby barnyard animals learn about the busy life of a farm. Cows are milked each morning, sheep are sheared for wool and horses are used for riding. As the baby animals grow, they will take part in the work, too.

Kids

Piglets

Baby goats are called kids and are full of energy. They love to run and play in the pasture. Piglets squeal anxiously for their mother's milk. They drink until they are full and then fall asleep.

Baby birds, yet too young to fly, wait for their parents to fly back to them with food. Someday they will be big enough to fly themselves.

Robin nestlings

Eaglets

Sea otter pup

Sea lion pups

Dolphin calf

Some baby animals make the ocean their home. They must learn to dive below the water and come up again to take a deep breath of air. Baby whales, dolphins and sea lions drink their mother's milk under the water. Sea otter pups float with their mother on the water's surface.

Whale calf

Some baby animals are very tiny and helpless when they are born. They stay warm in a pouch on their mother's stomach. Until they grow big enough to come out, these babies get a safe ride with their mothers.

Koala young

Joey

Opossum young

Orangutan young

Flamingo chick

Tiger cubs

Lush, green tropics are a good place to raise these baby animals. Orangutans swing in the trees high above the ground. Tiger cubs below growl as they play. There is plenty of water for flamingo chicks to wade in with their parents.

Elephant calf

Zebra foal

Baboon young

Rhinoceros calf

Lion cubs

Learning scents is an important lesson for baby animals on the African plains. They can smell other animals before they can see them, find watering holes and sense changes in the weather.

Antelope ca

Ostrich chick

Cheetah cubs

Giraffe calf

Hippopotamus calves

At the watering hole, many different African animals meet. Water has a long way to go up a giraffe's neck. One way to beat the heat is to stay in the water all day long.

Beaver kits

Bear cubs

Red fox cubs

Many baby animals are born in the spring and spend their first summer with their parents. While exploring the forest and streams, they learn the skills needed to find food and shelter for their first winter.

Woodpecker
chicks

Moose calf

Raccoon
cubs

Fawn

Skunk young

Caribou calf

Musk ox calf

Snowy owl fledglings

Polar bear cubs

Arctic fox cubs

Penguin chick

Seal pup

Animals in cold places of the world have especially warm coats. Some have fur that is thick and heavy. Others store fat to hold back the chill. Many baby animals' coats are as white as snow so that they cannot be easily seen.

PET STORE

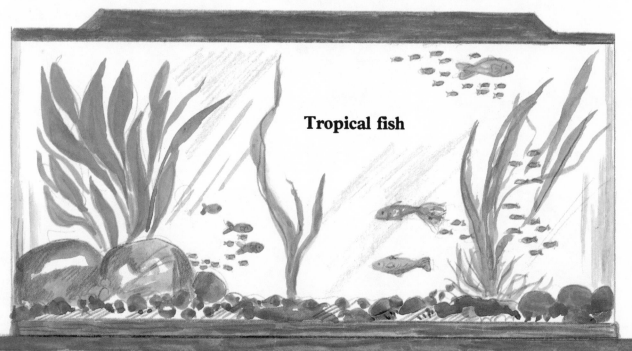

Tropical fish

Puppies

Baby animals in the wild have parents to care for them. Pets need people. With your care and love, many baby animals will make fine pets.

Parrot chicks

Hamster young

Rabbit kits

Kittens

Panda cubs

Camel calf

There are many different baby animals. Some are born tall while others are tiny and helpless. There are animals with spotted coats and others with long, shaggy fur. Some babies live in the cool mountains and some live in the dry desert. Each baby animal is special and beautiful in its own way.